THE DELANY SISTERS'
BOOK OF EVERYDAY WISDOM

ALSO BY SARAH AND A. ELIZABETH DELANY
AND AMY HILL HEARTH

Having Our Say:
The Delany Sisters' First 100 Years

The

DELANY SISTERS'

BOOK OF EVERYDAY WISDOM

Sarah and

A. Elizabeth Delany

with

Amy Hill Hearth

KODANSHA INTERNATIONAL
New York • Tokyo • London

Kodansha America, Inc.
575 Lexington Avenue, New York, New York 10022, U.S.A.
Kodansha International Ltd.
17-14 Otowa 1-chome, Bunkyo-ku, Tokyo 112, Japan

First published in hardcover in 1994 by Kodansha America, Inc.
Copyright © 1994 Having Our Say Again, Inc.
All rights reserved.

First paperback edition

Photographs of Delany's Delights tin (42) and soap and washboard (66) ©
1994 Jennifer Coates. Photographs of Delany sisters at church bazaar
(15), performing yoga exercises (110), and preparing garlic (108) © 1993
Daily News/Gerald Herbert. Photograph of Delany sisters with Regis
Philbin and Kathie Lee Gifford (104) © 1994 Steve Friedman/Buena
Vista Television. All other photographs © 1994 Having Our Say Again,
Inc.

LIBRARY OF CONGRESS CATALOGING-IN-PUBLICATION DATA

Delaney, Sarah Louise, 1889-
      The Delany sisters' book of everyday wisdom / Sarah and A. Eliza-
beth Delany with Amy Hill Hearth.
            p.   cm.
      ISBN 1-56836-042-8
      ISBN 1-56836-166-1 (pbk.)
      1. Delaney, Sarah Louise, 1889- —Quotations. 2. Delany, Annie
Elizabeth, 1891- —Quotations. 3. Life skills—Handbooks, manuals,
etc.   4.   Conduct   of   life—Quotations,   maxims,   etc.   5.   Afro-
Americans—Life skills guides—Quotations, maxims, etc.
      I. Delaney, Annie Elizabeth, 1891-   . II. Hearth, Amy Hill, 1958-
III. Title.
      E185.96.D368   1994
      973'.0496073'00922—dc20   94-34144

The text of this book was set in Janson Text

The jacket was printed by Phoenix Color Corporation,
Hagerstown, Maryland

Printed and bound by Quebecor Printing/Fairfield,
Fairfield, Pennsylvania

PRINTED IN THE UNITED STATES OF AMERICA

03 04 05 06   10 9 8 7 6 5 4 3 2

Dedicated to Our Sisters
Julia Delany Bourne (1893-1974)
Laura Delany Murrell (1903-1993)
Helen Hill Kotzky

CONTENTS

Acknowledgments   viii
Preface   ix
Prologue   3

1
OLD WAYS, NEW WAYS \ 9

2
LESSONS IN LIVING \ 23

3
STANDING ON YOUR OWN \ 35

4
LEANIN' ON THE LORD \ 47

5
THEY DON'T HAVE
POCKETS IN HEAVEN \ 55

6
FIRST THINGS FIRST \ *67*

7
HOMEFOLKS \ *81*

8
A HEAP OF TROUBLE \ *91*

9
SOUND OF BODY,
PURE OF HEART \ *105*

10
AIN'T GETTIN' NO YOUNGER \ *117*

The Last Word 131

ACKNOWLEDGMENTS

*T*he authors would like to thank Daniel A. Strone, Blair A. Hearth, Minato Asakawa, Paul De Angelis, Gillian Jolis, and Trigg Robinson for their advice and support in creating this book; Denise Landis for reviewing the recipes; and Elisa Petrini for friendly words.

PREFACE

"*It's* as if we've become America's grandmas," Sadie Delany said with a huge smile as we looked through a new basketful of fan mail. Now 105 years old, Sadie Delany, along with her "little" sister Bessie, 103, have become everyone's favorite centenarians.

Charming, candid, and oh-so-wise, the Delany sisters struck a chord in 1993 with their critically acclaimed memoir, *Having Our Say: The Delany Sisters' First 100 Years*. ("Twenty-eight weeks on *The New York Times* best-seller list—not bad for two old inkydinks over one hundred years old!" Bessie Delany is fond of joking.)

People often ask me if the sisters have changed (or been spoiled) from all of the attention. The answer, quite simply, is not one bit! What can you say about two celebrities who still insist on making their own soap and whose main preoccupation is getting into Heaven?

Their lifestyle, too, has changed little. They still live together in their own home in Mt. Vernon, New York. Great effort has been made to protect their privacy. Yet while the sisters enjoy living quietly, they have thoroughly enjoyed the excitement created by the success of *Having Our Say*. "We've had a ball," Bessie likes to say. And the Delany sisters are thrilled, yet overwhelmed, by the mail they've received.

When the letters came pouring in from readers, they often came with questions. People wanted advice, direction, and encouragement. The way they were raised, the sisters believed they had to answer each and every letter. But what to do? If they lived thirty more years, they would not be able to answer them all.

One day it occurred to the Delany sisters that in lieu of answering the fan mail, we could do another book together. Only this time we would not tell the story of the sisters' lives, but the secrets of old age.

Fortunately, I had kept a journal during the past few years, where I had jotted down the words of advice, parables, and amusing anecdotes that the sisters had passed on to me. We used my journal as a framework, expanding on the entries. Additionally, during the spring and summer of 1994, I prompted the sisters for new thoughts and ideas and wrote them down. As in *Having Our Say*, the sequence of material in the final manuscript is mine, but the words are all theirs.

—AMY HILL HEARTH
Westchester County, New York
September 1994

The Delany Sisters' Book of Everyday Wisdom

PROLOGUE

$\mathcal{W}$e are the children of a slave. There aren't too many of us left these days.

We were born more than 100 years ago and have lived together all of our lives. Our father, Henry B. Delany, was born a slave on a plantation in Georgia in the year 1858. He met our mama, Miss Nanny Logan, while they were attending Saint Augustine's, a school for Negroes in Raleigh, North Carolina. Mama was an issue-free Negro, which meant she was born free.

Mama and Papa were married at the chapel at Saint Aug's back in 1886 and brought up all ten of us children right on the campus. Papa was an Episcopal priest who served as vice principal of the school (they wouldn't let him be principal because he was a Negro). Mama taught cooking and served as the matron of the school—she ran the day-to-day operations. Papa eventually became the first elected Negro bishop of the Episcopal Church in America.

We didn't have one penny—not one penny—when we were growing up, but we had a blessed childhood. We had a good time, though we were very sheltered. In those days, colored girls couldn't go anywhere without a chaperone. Something bad could happen to you and there wasn't a thing your papa could do about it.

We remember life before Jim Crow Laws were passed in Raleigh in the 1890s. White folks and Negroes mixed together kind of naturally before that. But some nasty white folks—we used to call them "rebby boys," which is probably short for "rebel"—managed to get these Jim Crow Laws passed that set colored folks back a million years. You couldn't use the white folks' library. You had to sit in the *back* of the trolley. You couldn't use the white folks' restroom, which was the one that was kept clean.

God was the center of our Christian home. We had prayers morning and evening, and every night before Mama bathed us, we'd go into Papa's study and he'd read to us from the Bible.

After religion and family life, the most important thing in our lives was education. Back in the 1890s, colored children did not get much chance for an education. Since we grew up on the campus of Saint Aug's, we had a big advantage. At that time, Saint Aug's was a school for teachers and ministers. Because our papa was vice principal, we even got to take some of the classes that were meant for the ministers—like Greek and Latin!

When we graduated from Saint Aug's (Sadie in 1910 and Bessie in 1911), our degree was the equivalent of two years of college today. We were qualified to teach school, but Papa gave us this big speech about getting a four-year degree. He said, "Daughters, you are college material. You owe it to your nation, your race, and yourself to go. And if you don't, then shame on you!"

The only problem was that Papa had no money. And he insisted that we not take scholarships, because he said we'd be beholden to the folks who gave us the money. So what we had to do was pay our own way.

Now that was a mighty big task, but we set out to do it. Both of us worked as teachers down South for eight years until we had enough money to move to New York City and enroll at Columbia University. We each earned advanced degrees (Sadie in education and Bessie in dental surgery). Meanwhile, all but one of our sisters and brothers moved to New York, too. Lemuel, a physician, stayed behind.

Like a lot of Negroes around the time of the First World War, we were moving north in search of opportunity. There was so much racial prejudice in the South that we could not advance ourselves the way we wished. New York was far from perfect, but it was better.

We settled in Harlem, which was a beehive of activity. During the 1920s and early 1930s, it was the home of what they called the Harlem Renaissance: There were famous writers like Langston Hughes and musicians like Duke Ellington. The movers and shakers of Negro America, like Dr. W.E.B. Du Bois, the great Negro intellectual, all walked the streets of Harlem.

You couldn't help but mingle with these folks. And in the middle of it all were the Delanys!

Our brother Hap was also a dentist, and he and Bessie shared an office at the corner of Seventh Avenue and 135th Street, which became one of the hot gathering spots in Harlem. One of Bessie's patients was James Weldon Johnson, the first executive secretary of the National Association for the Advancement of Colored People (NAACP). Our brothers Lucius and Hubert were attorneys; Hubert was an assistant U.S. district attorney and, eventually, a judge. There were also our two sisters, Julia, a graduate of The Juilliard School of Music, and Laura, a teacher who graduated from Hunter College. And there was Manross, who was a career army man and businessman, and the baby, Sam, who owned a well-known funeral parlor.

They used to say in Harlem that the Delanys could take care of you from cradle to grave: We could take care of your health, teach you how to read and write, serve as your lawyer, and last, but not least, bury you!

Neither of us ever married and the reason is that we picked careers over men. You see, in our day it didn't occur to anyone that you could be married *and* have a career. It was one or the other. And the further along we got in our careers, the more we realized we did not want to give them up.

The two of us decided, well, we had a mighty nice time living together. After all, we were only two years apart and had always been together anyway. So it was just us two girls until Papa died in 1928 and Mama moved in with us.

After World War Two, we left Harlem and moved to the Bronx—it was like the country then—so that Mama could have a little cottage with a porch and a garden. We wanted the best for Mama. She was a joy to us.

In 1956, Mama went to Glory and it just about broke our hearts. But she was ninety-five years old, and we had to accept that she had to go sometime. We were so lonesome for her that we moved farther north, to Mt. Vernon. We figured we'd better start over or we'd never get past Mama's leaving us.

That's why we bought this house and have lived in it ever since. It's a quiet spot with a view of New York City and plenty of room for a garden. Yes, it was the perfect spot to retire. Of course, we didn't know we'd be retired *this long*! It's a good thing we found a nice place because we sure have been here awhile.

For about the last thirty-five years, things were mighty quiet. We had a pleasant life, working in the garden, going to church, visiting with friends and neighbors. We took good care of ourselves, doing yoga exercises every morning—except Sunday—and eating carefully. We eat a whole lot of vegetables and fruits and take vitamin supplements.

Then the funniest thing happened: We were discovered! This little gal named Amy Hill Hearth wrote a story about us for *The New York Times*. A book publisher read Amy's article and approached the three of us about doing a book together. Well, we thought we weren't special enough, but Amy convinced us.

We decided to call the book *Having Our Say* because Bessie would keep saying "Well, we're having our say!" as we worked on it. We didn't expect too many people to be interested in it, but it was a best-seller!

Now it seems like the whole world has been writing to us—it seems that a lot of folks, especially young ones, don't know how to live right. We're as old as Moses, so maybe we have learned a few things along the way, and we'd like to pass them on. We hope you find them useful.

—SADIE & BESSIE DELANY
Mt. Vernon, New York
September 1994

1

OLD WAYS, NEW WAYS

Sadie: So you want to live to be 100. Well, start with this: No smoking, no drinking, no chewing. And always clean your plate.

Well, you can drink a little bit, but not much!

We get up with the sun, and the first thing we do is exercise. God gave you only one body, so you better be nice to it. Exercise, because if you don't, by the time you're our age, you'll be pushing up daisies.

Most folks think getting older means giving up, not trying anything new. Well, we don't agree with that. As long as you can see each day as a chance for something new to happen, something you never experienced before, you will stay young. Why, we don't feel that we're 105 and 103—we feel half that old! Even after a century of living, we haven't tried everything. We've only just started.

But when you get to be our age, everyone keeps expecting you to die. That gets mighty annoying! One time a relative made a big fuss because we didn't answer the door. Bessie said, "I guess you thought we were dead. Ha! You'll see! I'll bury *you*." And she was right. We outlived her.

A few years back I had a physical and the nurse

asked my birth date. I said 9-19-89. She said, "That's impossible. *This* is eighty-nine." I said, "I meant *eighteen* eighty-nine." Well, she couldn't believe it. She said, "You're one hundred years old! Well, don't tell because no one would ever know."

Just recently, my doctor brought his little boy to meet me. The little boy had the same birthday as me—9-19-89—only the little fella was born in *1*989, and I was born in *1*889. The little boy was so excited to meet this lady who was exactly 100 years older than he was!

We never told our age until now. They say a lady who will tell her age will tell anything else!

THEN AND NOW

$\mathcal{P}$eople always ask us, "Are things better or worse today?" Well, some things are better and some things are worse. Doctors have more ways to help sick patients today. There's more opportunity for colored folks. But there are a lot of problems in the world today that no one ever dreamed of when we were young. For instance, this business about the environment. Why, clean water was just something you took for granted.

In the old days, another thing you could depend

on was the U.S. mail. Why, it was delivered several times a day! And it was faster. If we mailed a letter in New York by midnight, Mama would have it in Raleigh by nine o'clock the next morning.

That's because train service was generally good. Back in the 1890s, Grandma could cook a whole chicken dinner, pack it up, and take it to the train station in Danville, Virginia. It would arrive that same day in Raleigh, still warm, right on time for dinner.

Of course, there are some things that are more convenient today. Washing clothes, for example. When we were children, we didn't even have a well, let alone modern plumbing. So to wash clothes we had to start by going to the spring to get water. Each of us would take three buckets— one for each hand and one for your head. If you wrapped a towel around it for support, you could carry a bucket easily on your head. We'd carry our buckets back to the yard, where we had a great big iron pot and a tub beside it. It took us a few trips to fill them up. Then, using homemade soap, we'd scrub each item of clothing on a washboard. We'd boil the clothes in the pot to clean them, then rinse them in the tub. After rinsing them three times, we'd hang them up to dry. Lord, it was hard work but there's something satisfying about cleaning, as long as you're not in a rush. Doing the wash together, working in that warm, soapy water—it could be soothing, even pleasant.

Now today we have a washer and dryer. But washing machines are very hard on clothes, so we prefer to do most of our wash by hand. Our clothes last forever! We'll use the washboard and then put the clothes in the washer for the rinse cycle. We hardly ever use the dryer. We hang our wash outside on a clothesline or in the basement during the winter. When the sun shines on the clothes, it whitens them. And the fresh air is good for them too.

When we were growing up, we couldn't afford to buy new things, so it was important to take care of what we had. Why, we didn't even have a sewing machine at home back then. When Papa became the first elected Negro bishop of the Episcopal Church in America, Sadie made all his linen vestments herself. It took hours to sew things by hand, but they always looked so nice.

Everything took a lot longer way back when, but you know what? People weren't as frantically busy. Being busy is fine, it's healthy, it's exciting, but folks today just seem to zoom through life! In our day, people had to work hard, so they were tired. They were tired, but they weren't as crazed as folks today.

The two of us at a church bazaar. We haven't stopped having fun just because we're each more than 100 years old. Sometimes we still feel like two schoolgirls.

NEWFANGLED NUISANCES

Bessie: Folks do have some mighty fine gadgets today. For example, there's a gadget that allows you to open the garage door from inside your car. And these small computers that can do anything! Columbia Dental School didn't teach you a thing about bookkeeping, so I sure could have used one of those when *I* was working! And things like sandwich bags and wrapping paper are wonderful; we didn't have anything like that.

Television is an amazing thing. It can educate folks, and it can entertain. But now instead of reading, thinking, or just plain doing, too many folks sit and rot their brains in front of the TV. That's a shame, that folks would take something good and use it badly.

But there are some modern inventions we just plain hate. The worst is the telephone. Of course, when we were younger and I had my dental office, I had to have a phone so patients could reach me. But if you have a phone at home, you give up your privacy and hard-earned peace. Folks are free to bother you whenever they want. And people do all kinds of sneaky things by telephone. Years ago, we knew someone who would call us around five o'clock and say, "I'll be dropping by in an hour or so." Well, she knew we were getting our dinner ready and would feel obliged to set a place for her.

We know that phones can come in handy. We've heard of folks having telephones in their cars, in case they get a flat tire. That seems smart. But it's so much nicer to get a letter. It's permanent. You can read it over and over, thinking about what the person wrote, and when you write back, you have time to figure out what you want to say.

But even a letter can't compare to a visit. If you really care about someone, you want to see them, spend a little time together.

Some time ago several of our younger relatives ganged up and forced us to put in a phone. I suppose they were worried about us and wanted to be sure we were all right. They put it right by Sadie's bed. She just hated the sight of that phone—she used to keep it covered with her hat so she wouldn't have to look at it. And the *noise!* Why, it just kept ringing all the time, when we were sleeping or eating or talking to each other, so we refused to answer it. We don't need a phone to talk to each other or to the Lord. What do we need a phone for?

That phone rang so much that I began to fret. "You know, we'd better see what they want," I told Sadie. "Maybe something happened. Maybe somebody's up and died." So she picked it up, and—can you believe it?—it was a collect call. Someone wanted *us* to pay to talk to them!

That was enough for us. We'll never have a telephone again. If that's living in the past, we don't care.

Sadie: A lot of folks today are not in touch with the past, and I think that's a shame. Why, upstairs in our house we have a whole wall of family photographs that we've collected over the years. We feel so lucky that we have them. There aren't that many families that can show how they looked more than 100 years ago.

So when our young relatives would come visit, they'd always want to go upstairs to see the pictures, and, of course, we gladly gave them permission. Young people need to know their family history, and it's the responsibility of old folks like us to tell them. Anyway, there was one day that our young nephew came downstairs all upset. He'd just noticed that some of the pictures on the wall were of white men!

"Well," I said, "one of them is your great grandfather James Miliam, and the other is your great-great grandfather Jordan Motley."

But our nephew kept on fussing—about slavery and what happened between white men and colored women and oppression and what-have-you, as if it was news to us. How, he wondered, could we justify giving their pictures a place of honor? It's not that his ideas were entirely wrong, but they started to get Bessie riled up.

She said, "Those people are your ancestors, white or not, and so they're entitled to be up on that wall. You can't pick your relatives—that's the first thing. And the second thing is, those two men left us their land. If they thought enough of their colored relatives to do that, then they're okay by me!"

You can't change the past, and too many folks spend their whole lives trying to fix things that happened before their time. You're better off using your time to improve yourself.

THE COMFORTS OF HOME

Bessie: I'll tell you what I cherish most from the past: our family traditions, all those little rituals that bind you together. Folks today tend to be so busy and independent that they abandon the daily habits, like eating meals together, that keep you close. They think they can watch the TV during dinner or grab a quick bite and rush off. They think it doesn't matter. Well, they are wrong!

When we were growing up, we ate all of our meals together. Supper was the most special time, when we could talk about our day and just enjoy each other's company. It was comforting, and it was fun. Even now that it is just Sadie and me, it's still my favorite time of day. We make it a habit to have supper together—just to sit down at the table and talk. It's not until we're done eating that we bring up serious things, and that's when we make all our big decisions. Or if I want to tell Sadie that something's worrying me—and, honey, there's always something!—that's the perfect time for me to spring it on her.

I'd never give up our suppertimes. Folks who let the little rituals go are missing out on a lot.

FAMILY TIMES

Sadie: The family traditions I love the most are the holiday celebrations. I look forward to the planning, shopping, and cooking almost as much as the holiday itself. You know, you don't need a lot of money to make it special. Why, when we were children, the best Christmas gifts we got would seem cheap today—an orange in each child's stocking. When I think of Christmas, I can still smell those oranges.

For us, Easter Sunday was a holy day, so we'd wait until Easter Monday to have our fun. We'd go out to pick mulberries while Mama hard-boiled the eggs. Then we'd boil up the berries to dye the eggs the nicest shades of pink and red.

On the Fourth of July, Papa would light fire-crackers for us. He'd never let us near them because he was afraid we'd get hurt. Funny thing was, he was scared to death of them. Every time he'd light one, he'd toss it and run away like the Devil himself was chasing him. That made us laugh so hard.

Now, birthdays are something else again. We sure have seen a lot of them! Since Bessie and I were both born in September, we've always had a joint celebration. We got in the habit of celebrating on Bessie's birthday—September 3—because it was easier for Mama. School had already started by the time my birthday arrived on September 19, and Mama was busy. I never minded celebrating my birthday on Bessie's big day. I think it means more to Bessie, anyway.

Bessie starts getting ready the night before. In the morning she gets all dressed up. This is how Bessie got her nickname, "Queen Bess." One year on her birthday, Papa was laughing at her because she was strutting around and he said, "My, my, my. If it isn't Queen Bess herself." And she has to have her favorite cake: a pound cake with fresh coconut icing, served with a Boston cooler—vanilla ice cream in a ginger-ale float. She feels downright sorry for herself if she doesn't have that!

And she won't lift a finger around the house all day. But as she says, "I can't work—I need to spend the day celebrating. That's the least I can do to thank the Lord for another year!"

BESSIE: *The way we were raised, the first thing you do when you go home—straight from the train station—is visit the family plot. Then you unpack from your trip and see your homefolks. In this picture from the 1960s, I (holding the reins) am with cousin Daisy and her husband, Bigelow, going to pay my respects at Mama's parents' grave seven miles from Danville, Virginia.*

2

LESSONS IN LIVING

Sadie: You don't live for a century without picking up a lesson or two. Here's one Bessie taught me: That folks can't take advantage of you if you're doing what you want to.

When we were children, we all had daily chores. Each night, I'd wash the dishes and Bessie would dry, and our little sister Julia would put everything away. Well, Julia was always trying to bribe her way out of work. She'd say, "Bessie, if you put away the dishes, I'll give you a penny." More often than not, Bessie would do it—though she knew very well that Julia didn't have a penny to her name. I would ask Bessie, "How come you fall for that?" And Bessie would say, "Julia's not fooling me one bit. It's just that she hates her job so much and I don't mind it enough to refuse. Now she thinks she owes me a lot and, believe me, I'll get more favors out of her than I could buy with a penny or two!"

I've always been the kind of person who has trouble saying no. During the Depression, everyone needed money, and folks were always coming to us to ask for loans. Well, I made a mistake—I cosigned on a bank loan for a friend who didn't pay it back—and so every week, I let the bank deduct some of my check until I made up every penny. So when people tried to borrow money from me, I had a great excuse. I'd just smile and say, "I'd love to help you out, but you see, my wages are being garnisheed." That sent them packing, and I have to admit that today I still try to find ways to avoid saying just plain no.

If someone asks me a question I don't want to answer, I play dumb. I'll just say, "I don't know" or "I don't remember," though of course I do. It saves fussing, and I just laugh when they go out the door. Why should I care what they think of me?

THE SIMPLE TRUTH

Bessie: I just hate it when Sadie does that, though I have to admit that it works. Now me, I'd rather tell it to you straight! Papa used to say, "Bessie, if I ask you something, I know I'll get the truth." And he was right. I've always found that telling the truth makes life simpler and more comfortable. If you don't, you have to struggle to keep your stories straight, trying to remember what-all you said to which person. I could never stand the strain of that.

Besides, telling a lie is a sign of fear. It means

you can't face up to something. Mama always used to say, "If you tell a lie, you must ask yourself what you're afraid of."

I know it can be hard on people to hear the truth. As Sadie says, I can be too blunt. There's a young girl we know who had a baby on her own. I just hate to see a child grow up without a papa, and I can't stand the fact that she threw away her future on account of some no-good man. My opinion hurts her, but try as I might, I just can't hide the way I feel.

I wish I knew another way to tell the truth. You know, it ain't so easy being Bessie!

THE WEB OF LIES

Sadie: Although the truth can hurt, it's dishonesty that can do you greater harm. Here's just one example: When I was a girl, I got walking typhoid fever. Bessie came down with a worse case and had to go into the hospital, but I only had to stay in bed for a few weeks. Well, there was a girl who told everyone that she believed I had gone off to have a baby! She had a bad reputation herself, and so she tried to ruin mine. Can you imagine telling such a lie?

I don't think anyone believed her, but still, that hurt me. My good name means everything to me. As Papa used to say, "Children, all you have in life is your good name. If you lose that, you've got nothing." And it amazed me that the girl wasn't even scared she'd get caught in her lie. That's the thing about dishonest people—they can be very nonchalant about it or even proud of it. They lie to themselves so that they don't feel ashamed. If a person lies about one thing, you can bet, sure as I'm sitting here, that they'll lie about anything.

You might not always like them, but people who are honest are trustworthy. You know they'll keep their word. And as Bessie likes to say, "If you had a roomful of pennies in your house, it wouldn't even occur to you to count 'em when they leave."

THE HARD WAY

Bessie: I have gotten smarter about a few things in my old age, things like taking chances. Now, I know there are folks who are afraid to try anything new, and that's a big problem for them. But me, I was never afraid of anything. I mean, I was always absolutely fearless! Naturally that meant that I didn't always use good sense.

When I was young, we were just getting electricity at Saint Aug's, and Papa warned us not to touch the light fixtures. But I just had to see what all the fuss was about. So I climbed up on a chair and reached for that socket. Next thing I knew, I was glued to it! After a moment, I crashed to the floor. I was lucky I didn't get badly hurt.

Another thing we were told to stay away from was snakes. Of course, we had plenty of snakes in North Carolina, and I knew that many of them were dangerous. But that didn't stop me, no, sir! One day we came across a big old snake and, naturally, I had to go and pick it up. Well, it didn't bite me but it oozed something slimy on my hand and about scared me to death. It was horrible.

I guess I always had to learn things the hard way. I don't know how Mama and Papa put up with it. If there's one lesson I'd like to pass on it's this: Each of us doesn't have to reinvent the world. You don't have to try to do everything yourself. You can learn just as much by watching and listening as by doing.

Papa's favorite picture of Mama, taken about 1885. He carried it in his wallet until the day he died. Our mama was only one-eighth Negro and could have "passed" for white but refused to live a lie. She considered herself to be a Negro, even though her life would have been easier as a white woman.

Papa, around age forty, circa 1898. Some people say a great man is one who is wealthy and powerful, but our measure of a great man is how he treats his wife and children. On our scale, our papa was the greatest.

Sadie: Watching and listening—those are extremely important abilities to develop in yourself. Why, even when I was teaching, there were plenty of times when my students came up with better ideas than I had. And why shouldn't they? Just because I was the teacher didn't mean that I knew everything. No one can know it all.

Of course, there are lots of folks who act like they know it all. It's a shame, but there are a lot more big talkers in the world than good listeners.

Now, some big talking I like. Take Bessie—that gal could always outtalk anyone you ever met! She'd say, "If you can talk your way into Heaven, I'll surely get there!"

These days, Bessie claims that she doesn't talk so much anymore. She says she's tired of people disagreeing with her opinions. "I used to like a good argument," she says, "but now I don't care about fighting like I used to."

Well, you couldn't prove that by me! If Bessie ever did stop fussing, I'd miss it. I'd be worried to death about her. There are people in this world that God didn't make to keep quiet!

Bessie: I'd say one of the most important qualities to have is the ability to create joy in your life. Of course, at my age, it's a joy even to be breathing! Sometimes I joke with Sadie, "I sure am lucky that I'm so good at the things I enjoy the most—eating, sleeping, and talking!"

But when I was younger, I found joy in so many different things. My friends and neighbors. My church. And I dearly loved my flowers and vegetables. We filled our yard with them: wild plum trees, pear trees, fig trees, grapes, blackberries, raspberries, strawberries, African onions, leeks, corn, string beans, okra, squash, cauliflower, cabbage, tomatoes, and rhubarb.

There's nothing like a garden to help you appreciate the passage of time. In the spring, when those brave little crocuses and snowdrops poke up, we cheer them on. Then in March or early April come the daffodils. Then the tulips, and so on, until all the flowers bloom at once: lily of the valley, phlox, black-eyed Susan, cosmos, daisies, and, of course, roses. For some reason, we were always partial to red roses, so we planted more of those.

We never stopped improving our garden. Anytime someone gave us cut flowers as a gift, we would save the seeds and plant them in the spring. Here's a secret: If you're pressed for time, just drop dead flowers on the ground in your garden. The leaves and stems will become mulch and often the seeds will "take" by themselves. There's no need to ever throw out old cut flowers.

The plants I love most are the ones that come from little clippings we brought back years ago from down South. We'd just take a little snip and bring it back and root it. Why, we have a piece of our grandma's rose of Sharon growing right next to our front steps and some of her bridal wreath, too. And we have daylilies and iris lilies from the property of Mrs. Hunter, the wife of the principal at Saint Aug's when we were children. Having those plants is like having our homefolks here with us!

I love my garden so much that I would stay out there all day long if Sadie let me. That's what I mean by creating joy in your life. We all have to do it for ourselves.

Sadie: You know, my life has been filled with joy, too. My joy is Bessie.

To Lead a Good Life

1.

Never lose your sense of humor. The happiest people are the ones who are able to laugh at themselves.

2.

Pay attention to the little things. One of the best qualities a person can have is to be observant. Some people have eyes but they don't see.

3.

Think carefully before you promise to do something. Once you say you'll do it, you'll have to do it.

4.

Know when to keep quiet. When we decide that something is private, we'll say it's "graveyard talk." That means it's between you and me and the tombstone, honey.

5.

When somebody's nice to you, don't take advantage of it. You don't ride a free horse to death.

6.

Put your faith in the Lord, and you'll never be alone.

3

STANDING ON YOUR OWN

Sadie: People ask us how we've lived so long, how we got where we did. Well, the key is leading a disciplined life. If you're young, that means working or studying hard. When you're our age, it means exercising every day whether you feel like it or not. A lot of people cringe when they hear the word "discipline." They think it means having no fun. Well, that ain't true, and we're living proof! We have a good time.

Some folks today want to do things the easy way. We have a saying, "They want to get there—without going!" And there isn't any such thing. You've got to pay your dues. You've got to work for it.

Sometimes folks ask us how we put up with racism and sexism to get our advanced college degrees. How could we stand it? Well, what choice did we have? What choice does anyone have? Life's not easy for anyone, despite how it may look. Sometimes you just have to put up with a lot to get the little bit you need.

Now, it's true that you hear of basketball stars and entertainers making it big with no education. But that's only a tiny, tiny number of people. And it's sad, because a lot of them are too ignorant to know how to live well with their money.

If you are not educated—if you can't write clearly, speak articulately, think logically—you have lost control of your own life.

Dr. Anna J. Cooper at her home in Washington, D.C. All ten of us children were named after somebody. Mama and Papa had no money, and the only way they could honor someone was to name their children after them. Bessie (Annie Elizabeth) was named after Dr. Cooper, who was an educator and early advocate of higher education for colored women.

Bessie: When I was young, I told my papa that I wanted to be a nurse. He said, "Bessie, nursing is a fine profession, but why not try to be a doctor? Reach high!"

Well, I was short a few credits for medical school and I was running out of time, so I became a dentist—only the second colored woman ever licensed to practice in New York State. And I was a good one, I'll tell you! Why, just recently I heard from one of my old dental patients. I did a crown for her back in '29, and you know what? She still had it, more than sixty years later! That makes me so proud.

Pride in a job well done is the one kind of pride God allows you to have. I earned that pride. Nothing brings more satisfaction than doing quality work, than knowing that you've done the very best you can.

Reach high!

BESSIE: *I used to be known as Dr. Bessie, Harlem's Negro woman dentist. I never worried about catching contagious diseases from my patients because I had faith that God would look after me. I thought, "God didn't give me no gloves."*

SADIE: *Here I am dressed for horseback riding in North Carolina in the early 1920s. No matter how old you get, you think of yourself as young. In our dreams, we are always young.*

Sadie: Someone asked me recently how I handled students who failed. And I said, "Why, I never failed a student. Not in fifty years of teaching. I worked with the troubled students until they succeeded. I thought that was my job."

Doing quality work—that's what brings you self-respect and that's something folks seem mixed up about today. You hear all this talk about self-esteem or self-respect, as if it were something other people could give you. But what self-respect really means is knowing that you are a person of value rather than thinking "I am special" in a self-congratulatory way. It means "I have potential. I think enough of myself to believe I can make a contribution to society." It does not mean putting yourself first.

A big part of self-respect is self-reliance—knowing you can take care of yourself. When I started teaching school, I had hardly any money, so I came up with the idea of making candy to sell. Pretty soon, I had a little candy business called Delany's Delights, Inc. My hand-dipped fondant chocolates were sold in shops throughout New York City, including at the Abraham & Straus Department Store, in half-pound, one-pound, and two-pound tins. I charged two dollars a pound, and I made quite a nice little profit! But then the Depression came and I had to shut down my business because no one had the money for luxuries like candy.

Still, that candy kept me going for a long time! It showed me that no matter what happened, I'd never have to be beholden to anyone. Why, I've never needed a handout in my life!

SADIE: *My original Delany's Delights candy tin. I didn't wait for a man to come along and take care of me. I made my own money! I had a steady salary from teaching, but I also made good money on my candy business back in the 1920s.*

Delany's Delights
(SADIE'S HAND-DIPPED FONDANT CHOCOLATES)

First, make the fondant by boiling the sugar and water in a lightly greased saucepan to the "soft-ball" stage. Pour it into a pan, working it flat with a wide spatula as it cools, until it's creamy.

Next, take a small piece, about the size of the top joint on your little finger, and make it into a small ball. This little piece is then dipped in chocolate (milk chocolate is the most popular) that has been melted in a double boiler ahead of time. The room temperature must be kept cool. (I used to work with my coat on!)

To give the fondant flavor, grind nuts, soften chocolate, grate coconut, or add peppermint flavoring, mixing it into the fondant. Sometimes, you may want to use a flavor that can't be "folded" into the fondant (like whole cherries, pecans, almonds, regular peanuts, brazil nuts). In that case, you dip them, whole, in the fondant, and then in the melted chocolate.

3 cups sugar
1½ cups water
8 ounces
    chocolate (milk
    or semisweet)

OPTIONAL:
1 teaspoon vanilla
    extract or
    other flavoring

Bessie: Yes, folks today have got it all wrong. They've got this idea that self-respect means "I am a terrific person. I am wonderful. *Me, me, me.*" That's not self-respect; that's vanity.

But you do need to stand up for yourself. I'm the feisty one. I never took sugar in my tea, no, sir.

The way folks treat you often comes from the way you present yourself. That's why Mama and Papa taught us: "Always look people in the eye." If you don't, they'll think you're afraid of them, that you doubt that you're as good as they are. And then they're all too happy to agree with you!

There's a young boy who helps us with chores who just never could bring himself to look at us. He'd stare at the ground or around the room, mumbling his words, hunching his shoulders. So Sadie and I decided to make him our little project. We started telling him, "Stand up straight. Speak clearly—don't swallow those words." And especially, of course, we'd say to him, "Look me directly in the eye."

It took awhile to break him of his habits, but the change in him was amazing. His voice got louder.

His enunciation improved. His confidence grew. He even seemed taller!

You won't believe what finally happened. One day he came over and, standing proud and tall, he looked Sadie straight in the eye. And in a clear, strong voice, he offered her a deal. "For a dollar, I'll feed your dog every day. But all I'll do is feed him. I'm not washing out his dish."

Well, that sure made us laugh! Some folks might say we taught him a lesson that he learned a little too well, but we were kind of proud of him. We hope he carries that spirit with him for the rest of his life!

4

LEANIN' ON THE LORD

$Sadie$: For us there was never a time when we did not believe in God. There's a lot in this world you can't see that you still believe in, like love and courage. Well, that's the way it is with faith. Just because you can't hold it in your hand doesn't mean it's not there. A person who has faith is prepared for life and to do something with it.

When we were growing up, Papa kept the Bible in his study, and we'd get a reading from it every night before we went to sleep. Papa always handled the Bible very carefully. He used to tell us never to put anything on top of it, not even a piece of paper. It was sacred.

That Bible—the Word of God—was the center of our home, and you know, we still have it. We keep it in the living room, on a special small table between the two chairs where we spend most of our time.

The Bible is where we go for guidance. God's wisdom is at work in the words, but you can also get plenty of practical advice in the Bible. After all, mankind hasn't changed that much.

We find a lot of comfort in the old prayers and hymns, too. Why, one of the greatest gifts we've received in recent years was a copy of the old Cokesbury hymnal. It's a Methodist hymnal filled with songs we hadn't heard in nearly 100 years. Our papa was an Episcopal bishop, but his family had been Methodists. So when he got lonesome for his people, he used to play those old Methodist hymns on the piano.

Such beautiful songs, those old hymns, and the old spirituals too. With all the years of tradition behind them, they're bound to lighten your heart. Here's one that Bessie loves to sing:

> *What kind of shoes*
> *Are you going to wear*
> *Golden slippers*
> *What kind of shoes*
> *Are you going to wear*
> *Golden slippers*
> *Golden slippers, I'm going to wear*
> *Golden slippers, I'm going to wear*
> *When I go up to live*
> *With my Lord*
> *Going up*
> *Going up*
> *Going up*
> *I'm going up to live*
> *With my Lord*

Those old songs helped the Negro slaves, like our papa, survive; they kept them going. Those songs keep the Spirit in our lives.

Bessie: When we walk into our house—whether we're coming back from a long trip or just from seeing the neighbors—the first thing we say is, "We're home. Praise the Lord." We do that to honor Him, to thank Him for watching over us.

Of course, there are times when I wish the Lord *wasn't* watching, like when I run my mouth or lose my temper. I try to do right; I try not to stray. As Sadie says, "If you want to climb that ladder to Heaven, you've got to treat every day as if it's Judgment Day."

I think God understands that I'm only human. He gave me this mouth, He gave me a temper, and so I'm bound to err. I'm sure I must be getting credit for trying! But every once in a while, just to keep on His path, I try to take in an old-fashioned fire-and-brimstone sermon. I'm an Episcopalian, and I appreciate the thoughtful preaching in my Church—but there's nothing like fire and brimstone to set me straight.

Fight fire with fire, I always say!

Sadie: We set aside some time every day to talk to the Lord. We got that habit from Mama. She had a full-time job running the school, plus ten children to raise, but there was never a day in her life that she didn't reserve one full hour to pray. She had a beautiful writing desk where she kept her special things, like her own Bible and prayer book. Above it were two pictures of her heroes—Abraham Lincoln and Frederick Douglass—and when she sat down between them, we knew we had to leave her alone. That was her hour with the Lord.

Today we have Mama's writing desk in our living room and I keep those two pictures over my bed. They remind us that no one is ever too busy or pressured or tired to make a time and place for God in their lives. After all, He has to manage the whole world, and He's never too busy for us!

THE LORD'S WAYS

Bessie: I'm always amazed at the power of prayer. You know, I've always had trouble putting out of my mind and forgiving some of the mean people I've encountered in my life—you know, the bigots we used to call rebby boys. Then somebody suggested, "Pray for each and every one of them. Put them at the *top* of your prayer list." Well, I didn't like that idea at all. I said, "*What!* You expect *me* to pray for those nasty old rebby boys?" But recently I tried it. I just about choked on the words. But, Lord, it did make me feel better.

Sometimes I don't understand the Lord's ways, but who am I to question? I'm just a person, and I don't know why.

WE'RE IN HIS HANDS

*Y*ou never know when or how the Lord will take a hand in your life. Here's an example: In *Having Our Say*, we told about Papa's being invited, back in 1918, to give a guest sermon at Christ Church in Raleigh. The invitation was a great honor, and so our whole family came to attend the service. But when we got to the church, they stuck us way on up in the balcony because we were colored. They made us sit where the *slaves* had been made to sit. And then we were not given the privilege of Communion.

Well, after our book came out, you won't believe what we got in the mail. A formal letter of apology from the congregation of that church! We were so touched that they apologized a full seventy-five years later.

Now, *that's* God's work.

Bessie: Money is the root of every mess you can think of. There's some folks who would kill you for a nickel. Those are the sorriest folks of all.

Anyone who lives for money is surely missing the best things in life. There's satisfaction in doing, in helping. There's an old saying, "Money is useful, but don't let it use you."

Papa was terrible with money; he was *too* generous. If someone in the neighborhood back home couldn't pay his rent, he knew that Papa would give him the money. Finally, Mama had to take charge.

When people began to find out they couldn't get Papa's money anymore, they got mad. We had a cousin who said, "Your papa is so cheap that if the Statue of Liberty was shimmying, he wouldn't pay a nickel to see it."

I guess I inherited some of Papa's habits. Why, the whole time I was a dentist, I never raised my rates. So I'm always surprised today by what folks charge. A few years back we had a lawyer who charged a $150 an hour! Well, she came to our house and was carrying on about our garden and this and that. I cut her off. "Excuse me," I said, "but if you're charging a hundred fifty dollars an hour I can't pay you to chit-chat!" After our book came out, that lawyer asked if she could come by to visit with a friend. "Well," I said to Sadie, "if we let her, I suppose we should charge *her* a hundred fifty dollars an hour! Ha-ha!" We didn't charge her, of course.

I never had to charge my patients much because we always lived so cheaply. One time, Sadie read in a magazine about a woman who had figured out a way to cook dinner for her family for a $1.50 per person. And she said, "Bessie, I can surely beat that!" And sure enough, she did it for 75 cents per person. The trick is, you must cook from scratch, and you must shop wisely. For instance, we always buy what's on special. And once we're home, we store the food carefully so we never waste it.

Maybe because we were raised to practice thrift, we don't want to be rich! They say it's easier for a camel to pass through the eye of a needle than for a rich man to get into Heaven. We know the only thing money can buy that you really need is food on the table and a roof over your head.

Think about this: When I was a young woman, I went by boat on a trip to Jamaica. It was such a beautiful place! The sun, the flowers, the blue water. Everyone took it slow, enjoyed themselves. They knew how to live well! But you know what? So many of those folks wanted to come to New York. That was their dream. They wanted money.

All I could say was, "Don't you realize that you already have what money can't buy?" They had it in the palm of their hands and didn't even know it.

I'll tell you a story: Not long ago we went into New York City to be guests on a TV show. Well, those folks sent a limousine to pick us up. It was the biggest automobile we ever laid our eyes on. It was called a "stretch" limousine. We climbed in and sat way back at the end—and I just had to laugh. I told Sadie, "We could *live* out of this car!"

That was a joke, but it told the truth. People who care about things like limousines are courting trouble.

MAKING THE MOST OF THINGS

Sadie: We recently had to start recycling our garbage where we live. Since we never have much garbage, it wasn't a big problem for us. Any leftovers we have we give to our dog, and we reuse things anyway. For instance, if we use paper towels to clean up spilled water, we lay them out to dry and reuse them. We don't throw them out. We never waste a thing—not even things like corn cobs or watermelon rind. We use them to make wine or the best pickles you ever tasted.

Watermelon Rind Pickles

First, soak the rinds in salt water. After a few hours, peel the rinds. Then soak the rinds overnight in fresh water, in the icebox, in a covered pot.

The next morning, scald the rinds in boiling water for a few minutes, then cool them thoroughly. Put them in the icebox overnight again, covered with fresh water.

For 1 quart of pickles, heat up ¾ cup of sugar to dissolve in ¾ cup of water with the pickling spices. Pour over the rinds in a quart jar and let stand.

The following day, add ½ cup of sugar and ½ cup of vinegar. Bring to a boil, then remove from the heat. The next day, add ½ cup of sugar and ¼ cup of vinegar.

On the last day, add ½ cup of sugar. Simmer until the rinds are clear. Pack them into clean, hot quart jars. Fill with the pickling syrup to within ½ inch of the tops. Process for 10 minutes in a boiling water bath canner, according to the manufacturer's instructions.

Rinds from 1
   watermelon
2¼ cups sugar
¾ cup water

PICKLING SPICES:
1 teaspoon mixed
   (pickling) spices
2 sticks cinnamon
½ teaspoon
   cinnamon
½ teaspoon
   allspice
1 lemon, sliced
¾ cup vinegar

Corn Cob Wine

1 dozen raw corn cobs
1 gallon boiling water
2 packages yeast
9 cups sugar

Place cobs in a container and pour boiling water over them. Cover *loosely* with cheesecloth or a dish towel and let stand for 24 hours. Remove the cobs and add the yeast and sugar. Cover loosely again and let stand for 9 days. Strain through cheesecloth, cover loosely, and store in a moderately cool place until it is fermented, which may take as long as 10 weeks.

DON'T SCRIMP ON MAMA

Bessie: Now, there are a few things that are worth spending money on. For instance, when Mama was in her nineties, she needed special orthopedic shoes. Well, the man at the shoe store kept acting like Sadie and I were foolish to want to buy the *best* shoes for Mama. What he meant was, Why spend that kind of money on someone so old, someone who's going to die any day? Well, that made me furious! So we went and bought Mama the best pair, just like we had planned. We didn't have much, but giving Mama the things she needed—that was never a waste of money.

How to Handle Money

1.

When it comes to money, keep
your mouth shut.

2.

Cut back on your possessions. The more you
own, the more time you waste taking care
of things.

3.

Don't spend what you don't have. Forget
credit cards—they are the Devil's work!

4.

Don't live above your income. If your
income goes down, your spending
must go down.

5.

Out of every dollar, give the first ten cents to the Lord, the second ten cents to the bank for hard times, and keep the rest—but you'd better spend it wisely.

6.

Once you put your hard-earned money in the bank, leave it there! Smart people invest it, and then they'll always have some to fool with.

7.

Teach your children to save money from day one. Give your child an allowance so she can practice responsibility. A child who doesn't learn thrift at home will have money trouble all her life.

Sadie: Living cheaply isn't a burden to us at all. It takes a little more time, but there are some things—like store-bought soap—that cost a lot and just aren't as good as homemade. Why, I've never bought a bar of soap in my life! I made my own, and we use it in the bath, for the laundry, and even to wash our teeth! Even my neighbors swear by my soap. There was a little girl with sensitive skin, and her mother said my soap was the only kind that made her feel better.

If you make soap, here's something you have to watch out for. The last time I made it, I put it outside in the sun on our porch and Bessie noticed this neighborhood tom cat hanging around. She said, "Sadie, that old cat is sniffing around your soap!" I was afraid maybe he'd do something nasty to that soap, after we'd about killed ourselves making it. Don't worry; we ran him off.

Sadie's Soap

Some of these ingredients, such as lye, are poisonous, so be very careful handling them. Be sure to keep small children out of the kitchen!

Start by dissolving the lye in the 2 pints of water in a porcelain container. Set aside and allow to cool until the mixture is just warm. This may take a few hours.

Collect grease from cooking until you have about 6 pounds (or render it from fat bought from a butcher). Make sure you drain it through cheesecloth so that you remove any little pieces of meat. (Half solid fat and half liquid fat makes the best soap.)

Next, put the borax in a porcelain pan. Add the ½ cup of boiled water and the sugar and washing soda.

Next, add the sudsy ammonia. Follow at once with the lye and 2 pints of water,

6 pounds grease, melted and clean (or 3 pounds grease and 3 pounds olive, coconut, or other rich oil)
1 cup borax
½ cup water, boiled
2 tablespoons sugar
1 tablespoon washing soda
1 cup sudsy ammonia
1 can (13 ounces) pure lye
2 pints plain water

OPTIONAL:
2 ounces glycerin
2 to 4 tablespoons perfume, such as oil of cloves
2 cups oatmeal

checking first to see that the lye water is just slightly warm. Hold your hand over it—don't stick a finger in it. Then add the melted grease, a third at a time. Stir constantly until it's the consistency of thick cream. (Both grease and the lye solution need to be lukewarm to make good soap.)

If you're making facial soap, when the mixture is thick as honey, add the glycerin and perfume. Sometimes we add 2 cups of oatmeal run through a food chopper to give the soap texture.

When you're done, put the soap into paper boxes lined with freezer paper. When it gets thick, cut it into bars. Then put it in the sun until it bleaches white. Store for use.

One nice feature of this soap is that it floats!

Sometimes the old ways are still the best ways. You can't get clothes cleaner than with a washboard, and nothing beats homemade soap.

6

FIRST THINGS FIRST

*J*ust about every problem you can think of in this world could be solved in the home if folks were brought up right. There is nothing more important than having a good mama and papa, loving but strict. There were ten children in our family, but our parents were never too busy to reach out to the world. In fact, our family motto was "Your job is to help someone." Mama always said, "If it helps just one person, it's worth doing."

There was a student at Saint Aug's when we were growing up who was so homesick she would sit and cry. Her name was Josephine. Well, Josephine just wanted to give up and go home to her people. Finally, Mama said, "Why don't you come live with us?" And she came to live with our family and she finished school. And you know, she never left our family. She got a job working as a nanny for our brother Lemuel, who was a doctor.

That was the example that Mama and Papa set for us, and we've tried to follow it all of our lives. And you know what else they taught us? That color shouldn't matter. Why, when we were children, there was a white missionary at Saint Aug's who had a tiny baby with severe diaper rash. The woman didn't know how to take care of it. Mama told her, "I know how to fix that rash." So she took the child, bathed and powdered him, and in a few days he was fine. Mama took care of that white baby as if he were her own.

One time, when Bessie was studying dentistry at Columbia, she was with some colored friends and they encountered a drunken man who had collapsed in the subway. She stopped to help the man, and they said, "Why are you bothering with him? He's white." She said, "Can't you see he needs help?"

We don't see folks as black or white. This race mess is just plain foolishness! And the fighting that goes on between religions is crazy, too. Papa used to get very upset when he'd hear anti-Semitic remarks. He wouldn't stand for it. He'd say, "The Jews are God's Chosen People. Who are you, who couldn't make a flea, to disrespect God by criticizing the Jews?"

The world is full of nice folks, whatever their color or religion. As Mama used to say, your job is to find them.

$Sadie:$ I can't get over the litter on the ground in New York City. People eat a sandwich, they throw the wrapper on the ground. You might think that's a little thing to be provoked about, but it's not a little thing. It shows a lot about the character of the person, that he doesn't care about anyone else. It's plain bad manners!

We hate bad manners. By "manners" I don't mean using the right fork or spoon at the dinner table. All I'm talking about is performing simple acts of consideration, which sounds easy—and it is easy, but too few people even bother to try.

Here's an example: One day a friend was visiting us, a woman. While we were talking the doorbell rang, and our friend got up to let the person in. It was a man who lived nearby and—would you believe it?—he just charged right in and grabbed her chair. Just sat right down, leaving her standing there. Anyone could see that there was nowhere else for her to sit. He didn't even notice!

By the time he got up and left, Bessie was just steaming. She said, "Can you imagine someone being so rude?" But I had to point out—and she agreed—that it wasn't all his fault. He had what we call "poor training."

His parents are to blame for not teaching him the basic rule of courtesy—to be aware when you've inconvenienced someone else. If you get that lesson early, being thoughtful is a habit, something you do automatically. It's almost impossible for adults to learn that later on.

Our family in 1901. We're standing in the back row. Growing up, we had no money at all, but we had good parents, plenty of love, and a roof over our heads. One of the greatest joys in life is having a blessed childhood, and we have carried that with us all these years.

Bessie: One of the great gifts my parents gave me was a conscience, a real sense of right and wrong. That's not something you're born with. You develop it by watching adults, of course, but even more, you have to work at it.

Here's how we did it: Every night before we went to bed, Papa would tell us to be quiet and to reflect on our deeds of the day. Then he'd ask us, one by one, to confess all the naughty things we'd done that day. That's the first step—to be willing to admit your mistakes.

The next step is to ask the Lord's forgiveness for each error. Acknowledging them helps make sure you learn from them. And it keeps you from skipping over some!

The last step is still the hardest for me. I always say, "Forgiving is nothing compared to forgetting." It's bad enough to tell your failings to the Lord, but to apologize—I never *could* stand that! The worst was when Papa made us kiss and make up with our brothers and sisters. And to avoid it, why, I just had to be good!

You know, I'll bet that's why Papa made me do it!

SADIE: *I am third from the right in this picture of my graduating class at Saint Augustine's School, 1910. When you get an education, you don't just help yourself; you lift up everyone around you. And here's my diploma from Columbia University, 1920.*

THE·TRUSTEES·OF·COLUMBIA·UNIVERSITY
IN·THE·CITY·OF·NEW·YORK
TO·ALL·PERSONS·TO·WHOM·THESE·PRESENTS·MAY·COME·GREETING
BE·IT·KNOWN·THAT
SARAH·LOUISE·DELANY
HAVING·COMPLETED·THE·STUDIES·AND·SATISFIED·THE·REQUIREMENTS
FOR·THE·DEGREE·OF
BACHELOR·OF·SCIENCE
HAS·ACCORDINGLY·BEEN·ADMITTED·TO·THAT·DEGREE·WITH·ALL·THE
RIGHTS·PRIVILEGES·AND·IMMUNITIES·THEREUNTO·APPERTAINING
IN·WITNESS·WHEREOF·WE·HAVE·CAUSED·THIS·DIPLOMA·TO·BE
SIGNED·BY·THE·PRESIDENT·OF·THE·UNIVERSITY·AND·BY·THE·DEAN·OF
TEACHERS·COLLEGE·AND·OUR·CORPORATE·SEAL·TO·BE·HERETO·AFFIXED
IN·THE·CITY·OF·NEW·YORK·ON·THE·TWENTY·FIFTH·DAY·OF·FEBRUARY
IN·THE·YEAR·OF·OUR·LORD·ONE·THOUSAND·NINE·HUNDRED·AND
TWENTY

DEAN

PRESIDENT

CROWLEY, JAMES A.　　*Psi Omega*

　　Hoboken High School; Wm. Carr Dental
　　Society.

Another member of the gang.
Ah, Jimmy dear, your dome shines bold
But all that glitters is not gold.

DELANEY, ANNIE E.　　*Delta Sigma*

　　St. Augustine's School.

Way down deep
In one of the warm
Remote corners of all our hearts
We shall carry with us
Into the prosaic practical
World of Dentistry,
The memory of
A perfect lady,
Bessie Delaney.

1923

BESSIE: *Here are my yearbook picture and Notice of Completion from Columbia School of Dental and Oral Surgery, 1923. I was the only Negro woman in my dental school class, and I was mighty lonely, but I didn't let that stop me. I wanted to be the best dentist that ever lived. People said, "But she's a woman; she's colored," and I said, "<u>Ha!</u> Just you wait and see."*

College of Dental and Oral Surgery of N. Y.

302-6 East 35th Street

New York

Miss Annie E. Delaney　　June 1, 1923

Dear Madam:-

　　　　　　You are herewith notified that your work for
the Senior .....year has been............satisfactory and has been
accepted........... by the Faculty.

　　　　　　Yours truly,

　　　　　　Worthington Purcell

　　　　　　SECRETARY OF THE FACULTY.

Our family on a rooftop in Harlem during the 1920s. A measure of a close family is how much the children stay in touch when they're grown. There were ten of us, and all but one moved to Harlem after World War One. They used to say about us Delanys: "You never see <u>one</u>. Where there's one, there's <u>two</u>."

*B*etween caring for our brothers and sisters and all the children we've helped over the years, we feel like we've raised the whole world!

Sadie: I was always a softie when it came to children. I found out early that if I was kind, they would do anything for me. But being kind doesn't mean being permissive. Children need to learn discipline and responsibility. People used to ask Mama, "Why is it that your girls never seem to be in any trouble?" And Mama used to say, "I keep them *busy.*"

If you live right, chances are your children will, too. But teach them *everything*. What you don't teach them, someone else will—and you may not like those lessons!

Bessie: What children need most is love and attention. That doesn't mean spoiling them or letting them boss you. That doesn't mean letting them do what *they* want to do. But just sit with them, listen to them, look at them. A lot of people don't even *look* at their children.

The most important thing is to teach your child compassion. A complete human being is one who can put himself in another's shoes.

A WORD ON BITTERNESS

*N*egro parents should be careful not to fill their children's hearts with anger. If your child runs into prejudice, just tell 'em, "The world can be a mighty mean place sometimes." And give 'em a big hug and just go on.

It's understandable that colored folks are bitter. The only problem is, their bitterness won't change a thing. It will ruin *their* lives. If we'd been bitter and full of hate, we'd never have lived the pleasant life we've lived. Sometimes we get mad, but there's a big difference between anger and bitterness.

As Papa used to say, "They can segregate you but they can't control your mind. Your mind's still yours, no matter what they do."

*P*eople who intermarry tend to worry a lot about their children. They're afraid their children will have to choose between the races, that they'll have what they call an "identity crisis."

Well, we're part white and part Negro—our mama was mostly white—but we don't have any identity crisis. We're just ourselves, that's all! We're proud of who we are. We think of ourselves as colored people.

So we don't see anything wrong with interracial relationships. If two people can find happiness in this world, who cares what color they are?

Our advice to parents raising children of mixed race: Don't let your children get the idea from you that it's a problem. Our parents didn't fret about it, at least in front of us. Maybe that's why we don't worry about it, either.

A Word to Young People

1.

Don't have babies before you're ready—and "ready" means being married! Raising children is the hardest work you'll ever do. It's selfish to deny a child its best chances in life, and it's foolish to deny yourself a future.

2.

Finish school. A diploma may seem just a piece of paper, but it's worth a whole lot more than any paper money in the whole world. No matter what happens in your life—if you lose your savings, if you lose your home—an education will let you start over. It is the one thing that no one can ever take away from you.

3.

Don't fool with drugs or folks who do drugs! They have nothing to offer you but trouble.

4.

Don't be afraid to fail. Even if you do, you're bound to learn something along the way.

7

HOMEFOLKS

Sadie: Homefolks. What are homefolks? The most important people in the world: your neighbors and kin back home. Or perhaps a very, very special person who is new in your life. It's a great compliment to say "So-and-so is just like homefolks!"

When we find homefolks, we sure appreciate them. We've always had a lot of friends, many going back to our Saint Aug's days. Some of those friendships lasted longer than most people stay alive. One of our special friends was named Elizabeth Gooch, or "Gooch," as we called her. She was a maiden lady who lived with her sister, just like we do. Well, when Gooch's sister died, Bessie said, "We'd better take the train and get on down there to Covington, Kentucky, to see how old Gooch is doing." So we packed our bags and went on out. Gooch seemed to be doing fine, but if she hadn't been okay, we would have brought her back to New York to live with us. That's the sort of thing homefolks do for one another.

For true happiness, you've got to have companionship—other people, preferably one key person—in your life. It doesn't have to be a husband or a wife. It can be a friend or, like us, a sister. You can confide in a sister, share your secrets, and talk over your troubles with her. If you have a fuss, you have to make up. With a sister, you know it's forever. We always say that we've never had one best friend except each other.

By now, we've outlived just about everyone we used to know, so many of our new friends are much younger than we are. That doesn't matter as long as you care about the same things and, just as important, if you have the same sense of humor. And you know what? Younger people can teach you a lot. They keep you up to date. So we'll take homefolks wherever we find them!

One day, we were talking about our age and how soon we expect to go to Glory, and it made one of our young friends sad. She said, "I sure am going to miss you two someday." Well, Bessie told her, "Don't you worry, child. If anyone messes with you, I'll just put the curse on them from the Spirit World!"

Yes, we know how to look out for our friends!

GOOD AS GOLD

Bessie: When we talk about looking out for our friends, we're talking about loyalty. That's one of the most admirable qualities in a person and—

yes, sir!—it's one of the rarest. I have to say that we've been mighty lucky in finding special, loyal friends. Take our friend Lulu. She came from Saint Simons Island, Georgia, and she was a nurse. Whenever there was trouble in our family, like when Mama took sick, Lulu would come to visit and help us out. We never even had to ask.

Lulu died recently, and her niece sent us two beautiful afghans that Lulu had just finished crocheting. The niece wrote, "I don't think anyone in the world would enjoy these more than you two." She was right!

If you find friends like Lulu—folks you can trust and count on to show up when you need them most—hang on to 'em. You've struck gold!

COMPANY IS KING!

Sadie: There's nothing more rewarding than welcoming friends into your home. We always use the back door in our house, and that's where folks we see a lot, like neighbors, come in, too. We keep the front door only for our guests. It's to honor them—to show them that they're special. When company comes, we drop whatever we're doing. Company is king for us!

We've always had friends and family coming by, more than we could handle. That's a compliment! Why, there was a time when we made four cakes every week to serve company. Two we varied, but one was always chocolate and the other was always a pound cake. Here's how we made it.

Sadie's Pound Cake

An hour or so ahead of time, take all of the ingredients out of the icebox so that they are room temperature when you start. Put all of them in a mixing bowl except the eggs and oil. Beat by hand, or low speed on a mixer, for 5 minutes. Next, beating at medium speed, add the eggs, one at a time. Then add the oil and beat for 5 more minutes. Pour into a greased pan and bake at 325 degrees for 40 minutes. Then turn up the heat to 350 degrees and bake about 20 minutes more, or until the top springs back when you touch it.

1 cup butter
½ cup shortening (e.g., Crisco)
2½ cups sugar
4 cups flour (3 cups cake flour, unsifted; 1 cup all purpose)
1 teaspoon salt
½ teaspoon baking powder
1 teaspoon mace
⅔ cup milk
1 tablespoon vanilla extract
1 teaspoon lemon extract
1 teaspoon almond extract
6 eggs
¼ cup vegetable oil

Bessie: You know, animals are some of the best companions you can have. One of my best friends is my little dog. He's a stray, he's no good, but I love him. I feed him part of my dinner every night. He always gets the best part, and I feed him *first*. But my little dog can be a lot of trouble. Why, one time I locked him in the basement because he was naughty, and you know what that rascal did? He chewed all the leather buttons off my best dress that I had hanging in the basement on my clothesline. And I said to him, "Those folks who owned you before, they were going to get rid of you. Maybe they had the right idea!"

But I didn't really mean that. I just had to give him a piece of my mind.

Sadie: Bessie's at war with that little dog. He bedevils her. When he hides, he won't come out when Bessie calls to him. I say, "Bessie, don't you realize? He won't come because he knows you'll punish him." So I call and he comes right out and hides behind me. That just makes Bessie furious!

But she always forgives him. Those two just

love each other. Sometimes I think Bessie loves animals as much as she loves people!

THE TIES THAT BIND

Sadie: You know, it's the simplest things that form the strongest ties between people—like shared memories, even silly ones. For instance, when we were children we had as a pet a black kitty with a long black tail that stood straight up. Bessie just loved to play with that cat but he'd always try to get away. One time when the cat was escaping with Bessie chasing after him, she called out to me, "Catch him, Sadie! Catch him by the *handle*!"

Another time, when Bessie was still in a high chair, Mama was feeding her while talking to somebody. Without really watching, she just kept putting spoonful after spoonful of food into Bessie's mouth. Bessie started getting flustered—she hates to be ignored—and I guess she'd had enough to eat. So she started saying, "Plenty, Mama! Plenty!" We still laugh about that.

These things happened over 100 years ago, but I still like to tease Bessie about them. You know, the older you get, it's the funny little things that bring you the most pleasure. You like to recall them over and over again. Those are the stories that make a family or a friendship, and I cherish them.

GETTING INVOLVED

Bessie: Some people, older people especially, tend to draw into themselves. They're afraid of getting to know their neighbors or they're not interested. They grow isolated. That's a big mistake! You never know when you might need other people, but you need to earn their help. You have to contribute to your community.

Papa taught us that. He was so thoughtful that even if it was cheaper to go someplace else, he shopped locally. Even in the days when a few cents made a big difference, supporting our neighbors was more important than the money.

The Bible says you should love *all* your neighbors. Sometimes that's not easy! The worst are folks who are nosy but don't share a thing about themselves. We had a woman like that living near us once. She'd come right out and ask you anything, put you on the spot, and store up opinions about you. Sadie just stayed away from her, but she drove me wild. Of course, I can be a little nosy and opinionated, too!

A little nosiness can be a good thing. We've been retired a long time, so we're home all day, and our neighbors are glad to have us keeping an eye on the street. Like if we notice strange cars or people who don't belong in someone's yard—chances are they're up to no good. We belong to what they call a "neighborhood watch," and if we see something fishy, we go for help.

Some working parents nearby don't want their kids home alone after school. Who can blame them? So we help out by having the children stop off with us. One child would do her homework on our dining-room table until her folks got home, and one day she got stuck on her arithmetic. So I said, "Bring it over here. Maybe I can help you." Why, that child was so surprised. She just couldn't imagine that two old ladies like us could know arithmetic! Well, we showed her what to do, and the lesson she got that day was a lot more valuable than arithmetic. She learned to be more open-minded about people, not to assume, not to judge.

So we do our little bit. Getting involved is satisfying. It keeps us busy and makes us useful. Everyone has something to contribute!

8

A HEAP OF TROUBLE

Bessie: Today, sex is everywhere, all over the newspapers and the TV. Kids hear all about it, and so they get interested in it early. They know it's something grown-up, so they want to try it. They get the idea it's the most important thing in life.

In our day, it was different. Everything about sex was deeply private. Why, even with as many brothers as we had, boys were a mystery to us. Our parents kept us apart—the girls had their own room and the boys had theirs. Your little cot was all you had in the world that was truly yours. No one else slept in it, or even sat on it during the day.

I remember one time, when I was eight or nine years old, I asked Mama if my little brother Hap could sleep with me. We planned to get up before dawn and go pick "cressie greens," or wild watercress. But even though we'd wake up half the family with us, Mama said no. It just wasn't proper.

When we got older, of course, we had our share of beaux. We didn't want to marry because we'd have to give up our careers—and we'd worked too hard to do that! One man who wanted me to marry him was Dean, a dentist from Brooklyn whose family had a house in Sag Harbor. He finally gave up, saying, "I guess it's just as well. Folks in your family live a long time while mine tend to die young. You could be a widow forever." And you know, he was right. Dean died when he was only forty-six years old.

And there was a physician from Philadelphia, Dr. MacDougald, who really wanted to marry Sadie. His first wife had died and he had a young daughter, who still keeps in touch with Sadie to this day. But marriage proposals or no marriage proposals, we always respected ourselves enough to act like ladies. In return, those men treated us with the utmost decency. A lot in this world has changed, but men haven't changed that much. Women would get along a lot better today if they maintained their self-respect and decency.

I'll tell you a funny story about decency. Not long ago, I pulled a muscle in my back while exercising, and when the word got out, one of our neighbors—a man—came over to offer me a *massage*. That's right! He wanted to rub my whole body, from my neck to my backside. I was speechless for once in my life. All I could say was, "Oh, no thanks!" After he left, Sadie and I broke out laughing, and I said, "That man is crazy! Ain't no man gonna rub Bessie Delany's back! I never let 'em do that when I was young, and I'm surely not about to start now, no, sir."

Sadie: We had six brothers, so believe me, we know a lot about men. Men always want you fretting over them. One time one of our brothers moved in with us. His wife had died and we felt sorry to see him all alone, so we took him in. Bessie gave up her room and he filled it with his stuff—man-type things like guns and other junk. That was hard enough, but he drove us crazy when he started getting bossy. He'd complain, "Chicken for dinner *again*?" We were so relieved when he remarried and moved out. We'd had just about enough of him.

But there are worse things that women have to watch out for. There are a lot of men who are out for only two things: intimacy and money. When our papa was dying back in 1928, Bessie had to rush back to Raleigh from Harlem by train. She was just closing the door to her office when this man, a friend of hers, showed up and asked for money. She said, "The only money I got in this world I need to go see my papa on his deathbed." Do you know what that rascal said? He said, "You must have more money than that. You work like a dog, you don't go out much, and you don't even dress well." Now she says she wonders why she didn't pop that old fella in the mouth. Who did he think he was?

We were good-looking gals and it always got us in trouble. Men are a heap of trouble, just a heap of trouble. But we don't want to say that men are always in the wrong. Women aren't perfect, either. A lot of them look for the wrong kind of men— good-lookin' dudes, men with money, smooth-talking operators. It takes a smart woman to fall for a good man!

There are not too many men in the world like our papa. In our home, Papa was the head of the household, but he always treated Mama with great respect. Papa and Mama had a lifelong love affair, the way it ought to be.

WHAT ARE THOSE
GALS THINKING?

Bessie: I'll tell you something: Women don't know how to put themselves together today. Especially those hairdos—I don't think too much of them. It's like gals look in the mirror and say, "Hmmmm, let's see just how ugly I can make myself look today." That goes for the white gals as well as the colored.

I really dislike that hairdo called "dreads." We had a young relative come to visit us who'd done her hair in dreads and she asked us what we thought. Sadie was polite. She said, "Well, you know I liked the way you used to do your hair a little better." But I told her the truth: "It looks terrible! God didn't make you ugly enough, now you've gone and improved on the situation!"

Women today aren't modest. In our day, women tried to dress well, in clothes with good fabrics and flattering lines. But now you'll see these gals in tight pants and short skirts—they show everything! And it seems like the bigger the butt, the shorter the skirt! What are those gals thinking? Then they say that men don't treat 'em right or that no one takes them seriously on the job!

Mercy! Those gals are crazy. In our day you could get in enough trouble with just the ankle showing, yes, sir!

THE RIGHT HUSBAND

$\mathcal{S}$*adie:* A lot has changed for women today. It used to be that women were very secretive about their pregnancies. Mama used to wear these big long dresses that covered up practically everything.

You could hardly tell she was pregnant until the baby was just about born. So recently we were surprised when we had a journalist visit who was very, very pregnant. Bessie whispered, "I think she's going to drop that baby! In our house! We better boil some water!"

We had no idea that women nowadays worked right up until their time. I guess we learned something new.

Of course, when we were young, it was rare for married women to work at all. But today, it's common, even for those with children. There's no reason that mothers can't also have careers. But to do that, you need to have the right husband.

A man who's too selfish to look after his own children, who won't give them his time, well, that's the wrong husband. That man is no better than an overgrown child himself. How can he call himself a papa?

Every child needs a papa when he's growing up. Why, we'd be nothing without our papa!

WOMAN'S WORK

Bessie: I'll tell you some other new things we've learned. In our day, men absolutely never did housework, but today you hear about men who help their wives. I say hurray for these men! You know, when we were growing up our brothers would try to cook, but they always made a mess and they weren't very good.

But recently I've seen that men can be excellent cooks. Why about a year ago, we went to a Japanese restaurant. When we got there, they gave us a private room. And there, right in front of us, was the stove. And a *man*, dressed in white with a white hat. He bowed to us, very low, and offered us a choice of chicken, seafood, or beef as the main course. Sadie chose the chicken because it's healthier but, naturally, I ordered the beef. I can't turn down prime rib, no, sir, since Sadie won't let me have it too often at home!

Well, that man cooked right in front of us. He was so agile, so quick, I was just amazed. Why, I never thought I'd live to see the day I'd have some *man* cooking for me.

$Sadie$: Bessie likes to joke but, truthfully, we've never believed that there was such a thing as "man's work" and "woman's work." Why, Bessie was an excellent dentist, a job that most people considered man's work. That always made her so mad!

I suppose I always liked woman's work. I taught domestic science, what they now call "home economics," but there was plenty of science in it, including the study of vitamins and nutrition and basic principles of health—that didn't make it man's work. I still love to cook, and I could sew beautifully. Those were skills like anything else, and I was proud of them.

I learned those things well because I was a mama's child—I just adored my mama, and I would follow her around the house and the whole campus, copying everything she did. I guess you could say that Bessie was more of a papa's child. She'd watch Papa fix and build things—he even installed the plumbing and electricity at Saint Aug's—and pretty soon, she could repair things, too. She was always stronger than most women. When the wagon came from town with supplies for Saint Aug's, Bessie would line up with the men to unload it—and I'm talking fifty- and one-hundred-pound bags of things like flour. And she was so good with her hands. Not long ago, she made picture frames for all of our family photos and carved them with lovely leaf and flower designs.

So we think it's silly to worry about man's work and woman's work. Do what makes you happy and be proud of it. But have faith that anything you set your mind to, you can do.

Bessie: So few women had careers in our day that you weren't judged by your achievements outside the home. Instead what mattered were things like the size of the stitches in your sewing—the tinier, the better—and by how light and fluffy you could make your dinner rolls. Well, no one was better than Sadie at that—her dinner rolls were the talk of Harlem! She made all different kinds, but this one was my favorite:

Bessie's Favorite Feather Rolls

First, melt the fat and 1 teaspoon of sugar in ¾ cup of milk in a small pan over low heat. Remove it from the heat and then add the yeast. Let it cool till the surface is bubbly. Move to a large bowl and add the eggs, salt, lemon juice, baking soda, and 6 tablespoons of sugar. Next, add the flour, a cup at a time. You must beat the mixture smooth after each addition.

5 tablespoons fat from cooking (such as bacon fat)
6 tablespoons plus 1 teaspoon sugar
¾ cup scalded milk
1 package yeast
2 large eggs, beaten
1 teaspoon salt
1 teaspoon lemon juice
¼ teaspoon baking soda
3 cups sifted flour

Cover and let it rise until it has doubled in bulk.

Then stir the dough down and, ideally, put it in the icebox overnight. Fill a greased muffin pan half full, and let the dough rise again until it doubles in bulk. Bake at 375 degrees for 15 minutes.

SMALL VANITIES

Sadie: You know, we still enjoy all the little things that go with being women. There's a young woman who helps us out around the house, and every week she does our nails. Since Bessie was a dentist, she has always kept her nails short, and I would never have dreamed of painting mine. But now I regularly wear a fuchsia pink polish that seems to go nicely with my skin, and Bessie's nails are as red as blazes.

Having nice nails is a small thing, but we enjoy it. It's a harmless vanity, and it really cheers us up! We sure appreciate the fact that our helper thought of doing it. That's why Bessie says she's so smart, not only mentally but physically smart.

And here's something you won't believe: Bessie and I just got photographed for a fashion maga-zine. That's right—at our age! They wanted to doll us up and take our pictures at some beach in New Jersey. Bessie said, "No, sir, I ain't going to some beach in New Jersey." So the photographer came to us instead, and they fixed up our front yard so it would look like a beach.

We dressed in fine clothes, got our hair done up, and put on a little makeup. We thought we were looking pretty good! And Bessie said, "Sadie, I feel like a little girl again, playing dress-up."

Later we laughed about it. Bessie said, "I think we've gone plumb jack crazy to do what we did today." And I said, "So what? It was fun."

WE AIN'T DEAD YET

Sadie: We're still enjoying menfolks, too! Recently, my doctor said to me, "I have a patient— a man—who is 102 years old. Would you like me to introduce you?" And I said, "No thanks, doctor. How about somebody your age?"

Then when I was in the hospital with a broken hip, Bessie came to visit me. A man there asked her if she fixed her own hair, and Bessie told him, "Why, yes, I do." "Well, it surely looks nice," he said. Bessie was just tickled to death over that.

Bessie: Well, I'm surely not too old to get crushes on men! One time, Sadie and I were on live television and the host, Regis Philbin, went and kissed me right on the mouth! That shocked me, but someone said, "You sure looked like you enjoyed it!" And I said, "Well, maybe I did and maybe I didn't."

Another time, we were being interviewed on *Good Morning America* and we could not take our eyes off one of the cameramen. He was a tall red-haired man with a handlebar mustache. Finally, I said, "Excuse us for staring, but we haven't seen a mustache like that since Teddy Roosevelt was president!" Later, someone teased us, "Aren't you two something, flirting with that man like that." And I said, "Child, we ain't dead yet!"

We're still making new friends. The world is full of nice folks, if you look for them. Mama used to say, "It's your job to find them." We found Regis Philbin, who surprised us with a kiss on live TV.

9

SOUND OF BODY, PURE OF HEART

Bessie: Folks constantly ask about the "secret" that has kept us alive so long. Well, that's something only the Lord can say! We try our best to preserve our health, and one way we do it is to watch what we eat and drink.

We start our day by drinking a full glass of water, followed by a teaspoon of cod liver oil and a whole clove of garlic. A whole, raw clove—that's right. Garlic is good for preventing colds, and it's good for your bowels. We chop the clove as finely as we can, then scoop it up with a spoon, and swallow it all at once, without chewing, to prevent odor. We wash it down with one glass of cold water, then one glass of hot water.

Then we fix our breakfast. In the past few years we've found that breakfast is our most important meal. It's our biggest meal of the day, and we eat it right after we do our exercises. We have a scrambled egg each, a hard roll, and fruit, along with a bowl of oatmeal. I mean home-cooked oatmeal, not that instant stuff.

We have a good meal at midday. Northern folks call that lunch. We southern gals call it dinner. We eat chicken or beef—although we love fish, we don't eat it much today. We worry about its being contaminated. In the evening, we make ourselves a big vanilla milk shake. It's not good to eat your big meal toward the end of the day.

Every day we take vitamin supplements: vitamin A, B complex, C, D, E, along with zinc and tyrosine. We vary the amount depending on how we've been feeling lately. For example, if I start to get a little tickle in my throat like I am going to get a cold, I take more vitamin C. Antioxidant vitamins are the best. We think it's *best* to get your vitamins

The two of us preparing the garlic; when it comes to health, you can't fool around. Anything worth having in life, you have to work at.

naturally, from foods you eat, but supplements are a good idea.

I keep saying "we," but the truth is Sadie's the one in charge of our health. She makes me take my cod liver oil—I can't stand the nasty stuff—and eat what she tells me. If she doesn't think I'm eating enough, she watches me. That just ruins my appetite altogether!

She drives me a little crazy but I guess she's doing something right! I have 103 years of living to show for it.

LIMBER UP!

Sadie: There's another thing I make Bessie do that she doesn't like too much, and that's exercise. You've got to exercise, not just for your heart and lungs, but to keep from stiffening up. It keeps you limber, and that's important when you get older.

We started doing yoga about forty years ago, but don't think we didn't get exercise before that! When we were younger and lived in New York City, we'd walk for miles because we couldn't afford to take the trolley. That was mighty good exercise!

We've been doing exercises every day for about forty years now, and it's part of what keeps us active. Here we're 102 and 100.

You don't have to get down on the floor and do yoga. You can get exercise from doing housework, gardening, all kinds of things—anything's better than sitting on your behind all day long.

GARDEN OF HEALTH

Bessie: Well, I always did prefer gardening to that old yoga. Why, to plant a seed and watch it grow is one of the greatest pleasures of life. We rarely had to buy vegetables because our garden was so lush. In the summer, we'd pick what we wanted to eat for dinner—whatever was ripe—and each fall we'd can a lot of them to eat all winter.

We just know that those vegetables keep us healthy. We make it a point to eat seven different vegetables every day. One way we do it is to cook up dishes that give us all of them at once.

Sadie's Seven Vegetable Casserole

Chop cabbage, turnips, broccoli, carrots, onions, celery, and cauliflower. Layer, one at a time, in a frying pan. Repeat until all the ingredients have been used up. Add a tablespoon of oil. Cook at low heat for 20 minutes.

Sadie: If you eat a lot of fruit, it will extend your life. Not long ago some fresh bing cherries brought Bessie out of a slump. She was feeling weak, so she ate a bunch before she went to sleep, and you know what? She woke up feeling 100 percent better! She swears it was those bing cherries.

We love fruit, but we've had to cut back on eating citrus fruits because we think they can aggravate rheumatism. But there's one dessert, ambrosia, that we just can't pass up. It was our papa's favorite. Having grown up in Florida, he loved his citrus fruit.

Our family has a funny story about ambrosia. One time, Mama sent ambrosia by train from Raleigh to her parents near Danville, Virginia. We used to do this all the time, but this time there was a delay and the ambrosia started to ferment. Grandma was going to throw it out but our grandfather said, "No, Martha, just put it on the mantelpiece." Oh, he was smart. Every morning he cut off a piece, and he surely did enjoy his ambrosia *liqueur.* It had developed quite a kick!

We always make ambrosia on February 5, Papa's birthday. It's a nice way to remember him.

Ambrosia

First, split open the coconut, peel the black skin inside to remove, and grate the meat with a fine grater; cover it and set aside. Next, peel the oranges, stripping the skin and the white membrane. Slice thinly and discard the seeds. (Mama's shortcut: Peel the oranges, but *don't* remove the white skin. Just slice thinly. Besides, the white skin is good for you.)

In a large serving bowl, place a layer of grated coconut. Follow with a layer of oranges. Then sprinkle on a handful of sugar. Keep repeating these three steps until the bowl is filled, ending with coconut.

Place in the icebox overnight, and spoon into parfait dishes for serving.

Meat of 1 fresh
   coconut, grated
About 1 dozen
   oranges
Sugar

Sadie: It's important to eat healthy, but you won't live a long time unless you indulge yourself every once in a while!

When Bessie gets a little blue, I go in the kitchen and fix and fix and fix until I cook something that old gal can't resist eating. I know all her favorite foods, you know. Nothing works like coconut to cheer up Bessie. Next thing you know, she's her old self, laughing and carrying on. She loves coconut, and that usually does the trick.

½ cup butter
½ cup shortening
   (e.g., Crisco)
4 tablespoons
   margarine
2 to 3 cups fresh
   coconut, grated
2 eggs
1 tablespoon
   vanilla extract
1 teaspoon lemon
   extract
3 cups flour
1½ cups sugar
½ teaspoon salt
½ teaspoon mace

Bessie's Fresh Coconut Cookies

Blend butter, shortening, margarine, and coconut. Add the eggs and the vanilla and lemon extracts. Sift the dry ingredients and stir into the coconut mixture. Make into medium-size balls, flatten slightly, and bake at 350 degrees for 20 minutes.

Bessie: Alcohol is another little indulgence that's okay, as long as you use it in moderation. It can help you relax and that's good. But we don't go in for that store-bought stuff. Instead, we make our own with the rose petals from our garden.

Sadie's Rose Wine

Take a 1½- to 2-gallon glass or plastic container and fill it with the rose petals (red for good color). Then add 3 quarts of boiling water and let cool overnight. The next day, add the juice and cut-up lemons and oranges and let stand for 3 whole days. Then strain it through cheesecloth. Add yeast cakes, sugar, and enough water to make 2 gallons. Pour into sterilized gallon jugs and cover loosely with cheesecloth or a dish towel. Store in a moderately cool place until fermentation ceases (at least 4, possibly as long as 10, weeks). Then pour into bottles and cork.

3 quarts rose petals from the garden

3 quarts boiling water

2 lemons, squeezed and cut up

4 oranges, squeezed and cut up

2 yeast cakes

7 pounds sugar

Bessie: Water, of course, is the most important drink, and so we're very careful about ours. Why, we'd never dream of drinking it straight from the tap. We boil it first to purify it, then when it cools down, we store it in glass jars.

That's what smart folks did in our day. Another thing we do is wash our hands the minute we walk in the house, the way Mama taught us. She was the cleanest woman alive! When we traveled overnight by train, Mama would get up before dawn to clean the bathroom until it was spotless. How we grumbled when she woke us up, saying, "Girls, hurry up! Get in there before someone else comes along!"

Those habits may sound funny, but they were critical back then, when there were no antibiotics to treat disease. All you could do was prevent it. We figure the world is just as dirty—or worse!—today. Why take a chance on getting sick? We can't remember the last time we had a cold.

Clean livin'—that's what we believe in. And hygiene's only part of it. We also try to stay pure of heart.

AIN'T GETTIN'
NO YOUNGER

Sadie: When you get old, everyone starts to worry about you. They say, "Don't do this, don't do that." It drives us plumb jack crazy. Bessie always says, "If I break my fool neck falling down the stairs while I'm feeding my little dog, well, so be it."

Folks think that because you're old, you're unable to do for yourself. Well, look at us! One time about ten years ago, when we were in our nineties, we needed to move an icebox from storage in the attic to the kitchen. We had hired two men to do it, but days and days passed and they never got around to it. Well, we just up and moved that icebox ourselves. That's right! Me and Bessie. We were slow and careful about it—the hardest part was all those stairs—but we did it. Those two men finally came by and said, "Okay, we're ready to move the refrigerator now." And we said, "You're too late!" They couldn't believe that these two old ladies had moved it themselves. We didn't need those men!

Now, I'm not saying that older folks should try to do it all without help. All I mean is that you can't let folks assume that you're nothing but a helpless old fool.

But you do have to be honest about your limitations. If you don't do that, well, your clock's not ticking right!

SADIE: *I'm about sixty-five in this picture.*
The Delany women always looked ten years younger than they were. It's a family trait. Papa used to say, "Well, there's no reason for anyone to know how old you are." He kept our ages out of the family Bible so that no one would peek. All of our brothers kept the secret. They didn't lie, but they always gave the impression that we were their <u>little</u> sisters.

Bessie: It is a nuisance when people keep worrying about us! But I admit that I do tend to worry myself. When Sadie was 103, she broke her left hip and landed in the hospital and, honey, *that's* a situation worth worrying about.

You know, showing up at a hospital at 103 years old, no one wants to touch you. They don't know what to do with old folks, and they just assumed we were senile. They'd talk in front of us like we weren't there. It was mighty insulting.

Well, they finally got a surgeon who would do the operation, which was a success, but Sadie had to stay in the hospital for almost two months. I was just worried to death. I *hated* that hospital. And you know what I hated most? I discovered that the morgue was so close to the kitchen! I'm sort of fanatical about germs, you know. I guess it comes from being a dentist. I like things clean.

But Sadie would say, "Now, Bessie, don't you worry yourself to death. This place isn't going to kill me! Let's just make the best of things." She's smarter than me that way.

Every day she'd remind me, "It's in the Lord's hands, so why fret about it?"

Sadie: My brightest moment in the hospital was the time Bessie brought my brush and plaited my hair for me. When I looked up, I saw three nurses standing in the doorway, just watching us. I guess they thought it was sweet, this woman over 100 years old brushing her big sister's hair.

I enjoyed that, and I did my best to get along in the hospital. Why, I even learned a few survival tricks. The food was always cold, so I'd order tea, but I didn't plan to drink it. Instead, I'd take the hot water for the tea and spoon it over the food, especially the sauces, to heat it up. It worked like a charm, and I got my hot food. One time the nurses got all upset because they thought I'd disappeared, but I was out in the hallway practicing with my walker. Nobody told me to do that. I just knew I had to take things into my own hands if I was going to get out of that place.

I kept getting roommates who were much younger than me. Funny thing is, I was in a lot better shape than they were! One of them, a lady who was probably in her seventies, was upset and frightened. Nobody came to see her and everyone at the hospital was too busy to pay much attention to her.

Well, I decided I would help her, advocate for her. I'd ring the nurse's buzzer for her when she needed something. I'd calm her down when she got scared. And I'd encourage her, saying, "Now, dear, you really must *try*."

That's a big problem with some older folks— they have such low expectations of themselves. When they get to a certain age, they just give up. That's a shame! If there's anything I've learned in all these years, it's that life is too good to waste a day. It's up to you to make it sweet.

SHOW THEM WHO'S THE BOSS

Bessie: When Sadie got home from the hospital, she was very weak, but walking with a walker. So folks thought that for the first time in our lives, we needed help at home. Well, I wasn't about to put up with *that*! I said, "No, sir. There's no one who can take care of Sadie better than I can."

One of my nephews tried to get me to do this and that, but I said, "You run your household; I'll run mine!"

And I did. We managed well for about eight months, and then Sadie broke her *other* hip. Then—can you believe it?—no sooner did Sadie get home than I fell and broke *my* hip. That's right! Now, honey, we're as old as Moses and I guess we should expect these things, but it's mighty hard when your brain works fine and your body is giving out on you.

You know, there's two places I never want to go. One's jail and the other is the hospital! So when the ambulance came for me I told that driver, "Just take me straight to the cemetery. I'd rather go there, yes, sir!"

When I got to the hospital, folks expected that I would behave like Sadie. Honey, that is the story of my life. Ever since I was born, I've been following in Sadie's footsteps. Why, back when we were both teaching, I got a job at one of Sadie's old schools. All I heard was "Sadie does it like this" or "That's not how Sadie did it." Finally I said, "Look, I'm not Sadie. I'm Bessie. And if you don't like it, well, that's just too bad."

The other time I was in the hospital was way back in 1906, when I got typhoid fever. I was just fifteen years old. But this time, don't worry, I showed those folks who's the boss. Oh, I was *bad*. I'd never let them poke and prod *me*! One day a friend who was visiting noticed my nails had gotten long and offered me a manicure. I said, "No, sir! Don't touch my nails. Why, I just might need these claws!"

Now, I'm not saying the way I carried on was

right. All those folks were just trying to help. Sadie gets her way by being sweet and determined but, honey, I don't mince words. If you mess with me, you've got a world of trouble.

But however you do it, you've just got to fight in this life. When you're young, you're busy trying to fight against all the big problems of the world. When you're older, you have to fight to hold on to things like your property and your dignity and your independence.

If there's one thing you've got to hold on to, it's the courage to fight!

A Word to Older Folks

1.

Keep your own calendar. The most important thing in your life is your time, and nothing will make you feel as helpless as having other people run it for you.

2.

Manage your own money, but be careful about it. Pay your own bills and balance your checkbook for as long as you can. When the time comes that someone has to take a hand in your finances, make sure you understand everything he does. If other people take charge of your money, it's easy to lose control of your life.

3.

Have your own doctor, who answers to you. If you don't, when the time comes that you get mixed up with hospitals, they'll treat you like a fool. One time when Sadie was in the hospital, a technician was taking her blood pressure, and Sadie simply asked how it was—good, bad, or indifferent? Why, that girl looked at her like she was crazy! "Indifferent," she said, like

it was none of Sadie's business. Well, we solved
that problem by getting our own woman
gerontologist. You're bound to lose your health
at some point, but you don't have to
lose your dignity, too.

4.

Don't depend too much on any one person.
If you have a lot of helpers, you can be sure that
someone will always be available when you need it.
You'll feel a lot more independent. We have
different folks who do different things for us—
like give us a ride, go to the post office, or
buy our vitamins. By spreading out
these little favors, we're not a big
burden on anyone.

5.

Don't be too proud to accept your limitations.
The hardest thing is discovering that you can't do
everything the way you used to. We're not happy
having folks help us around the house, but
we've come to accept it. But make sure you
hire folks who do what *you* want. It's still
your house, and you're still the boss!

Bessie: When you get older, it's natural to look back on your life. And like most folks, I have a few regrets. The main regrets I have from 100 years of living come from when I haven't treated someone as well as I could have. When we were children, we used to play near the principal's house on campus at Saint Aug's. His wife, Mrs. Hunter, would come out and very nicely say, "Now, children, Mrs. Hunter has a migraine headache. Please play somewhere else." We'd go off for a while but we always came back to her yard. Looking back, I'm sure we worried that poor woman to death. And you know, I still feel bad about it, after all these years.

And I can be a little mean. Sadie never says anything mean about anyone, especially if they're dead. If I say something mean about someone who's gone to Glory, Sadie will say, "Now, Bessie, of the dead say nothing evil," and I try to be good.

Mama used to tell me, "Bessie, someday you're going to have to account for every mean thing you've ever said." That's what's got me so worried. If I had to do it all over again, I'd hush up once in a while.

Sadie: I know this sounds hard to believe, but I don't have any regrets. I'm the type of person who tends to think before I speak or act, so I don't make so many mistakes . . . or so I hope.

When you get older, you ask yourself, "How have I run my life? Did I live it well?" I think I have. I'm completely satisfied. Maybe all older people should be asked about their lives. When you live a long time, you have stories to tell. If only people ask.

THE LAST WORD

Sadie: This is going to sound kind of crazy to some folks, but we aren't worried about dying one bit. We're hopeful that we'll get to Heaven. And won't it be the greatest pleasure to see Mama and Papa again?

Bessie says she's been to too many funerals in her life. "Next one I go to will be my own," she always says. You see, Bessie feels things deeply. She never stops missing anyone while I just pick up and go on.

She told me recently, "Sadie, I think I'm going to die in my sleep. I think that sounds pretty good." And I said, "Good for *you*, maybe! But what about *me*!" I think that would be a mean thing for her to do to me.

But you know, we aren't ready to give up yet, unless the Lord makes up His mind that it's finally time to call us. In the meantime, like all human beings, we want to keep on living. As Bessie says, "Heaven is my home but, honey, I ain't homesick!"

When our time comes, we're going to be buried in the family plot in Raleigh. Bessie and I will be buried side by side—right next to Mama and Papa.

We couldn't ask for anything more.